This Yoga Journal Belongs to

_____

_____

Yoga
is a form of
self-respect

#ILOVEYOGA

Month:

My Yoga Goals This Month

_____
_____
_____
_____

What Can I Do To Reach my Goals?

_____
_____
_____
_____

My Progress

_____
_____
_____
_____

Feelings After Reaching my Goals

_____
_____

Daily Yoga

Date:

Intentions/My Mantra

_____
_____
_____
_____

How Did I feel Before?

_____
_____
_____
_____

My Practice/Workout

_____
_____
_____

How Did I Feel After?

_____
_____

Daily Yoga

Date:

Intentions/My Mantra

_____
_____
_____
_____

How Did I feel Before?

_____
_____
_____
_____

My Practice/Workout

_____
_____
_____
_____

How Did I Feel After?

_____
_____

Daily Yoga

Date:

Intentions/My Mantra

_____
_____
_____
_____

How Did I feel Before?

_____
_____
_____
_____

My Practice/Workout

_____
_____
_____

How Did I Feel After?

_____
_____

Daily Yoga

Date:

Intentions/My Mantra

How Did I feel Before?

My Practice/Workout

How Did I Feel After?

Daily Yoga

Date:

Intentions/My Mantra

_____
_____
_____
_____

How Did I feel Before?

_____
_____
_____
_____

My Practice/Workout

_____
_____
_____

How Did I Feel After?

_____
_____

Daily Yoga

Date:

Intentions/My Mantra

_____
_____
_____
_____

How Did I feel Before?

_____
_____
_____
_____

My Practice/Workout

_____
_____
_____
_____

How Did I Feel After?

_____
_____

Daily Yoga

Date:

Intentions/My Mantra

_____
_____
_____
_____

How Did I feel Before?

_____
_____
_____
_____

My Practice/Workout

_____
_____
_____
_____

How Did I Feel After?

_____
_____

Daily Yoga

Date:

Intentions/My Mantra

_____
_____
_____
_____

How Did I feel Before?

_____
_____
_____

My Practice/Workout

_____
_____
_____
_____

How Did I Feel After?

_____
_____

Daily Yoga

Date: _____

Intentions/My Mantra

_____
_____
_____
_____

How Did I feel Before?

_____
_____
_____
_____

My Practice/Workout

_____
_____
_____
_____

How Did I Feel After?

_____
_____

Daily Yoga

Date:

Intentions/My Mantra

_____

_____

_____

_____

How Did I feel Before?

_____

_____

_____

_____

My Practice/Workout

_____

_____

_____

_____

How Did I Feel After?

_____

_____

Daily Yoga

Date:

Intentions/My Mantra

_____
_____
_____
_____

How Did I feel Before?

_____
_____
_____
_____

My Practice/Workout

_____
_____
_____
_____

How Did I Feel After?

_____
_____

Daily Yoga

Date:

Intentions/My Mantra

_____

_____

_____

_____

How Did I feel Before?

_____

_____

_____

_____

My Practice/Workout

_____

_____

_____

How Did I Feel After?

_____

_____

Daily Yoga

Date:

Intentions/My Mantra

_____
_____
_____
_____

How Did I feel Before?

_____
_____
_____
_____

My Practice/Workout

_____
_____
_____
_____

How Did I Feel After?

_____
_____

Daily Yoga

Date:

Intentions/My Mantra

_____
_____
_____
_____

How Did I feel Before?

_____
_____
_____
_____

My Practice/Workout

_____
_____
_____
_____

How Did I Feel After?

_____
_____

Daily Yoga

Date:

Intentions/My Mantra

_____
_____
_____
_____

How Did I feel Before?

_____
_____
_____
_____

My Practice/Workout

_____
_____
_____

How Did I Feel After?

_____
_____

Daily Yoga

Date:

Intentions/My Mantra

How Did I feel Before?

My Practice/Workout

How Did I Feel After?

Daily Yoga

Date:

Intentions/My Mantra

_____

_____

_____

_____

How Did I feel Before?

_____

_____

_____

_____

My Practice/Workout

_____

_____

_____

_____

How Did I Feel After?

_____

_____

_____

Daily Yoga

Date:

Intentions/My Mantra

_____
_____
_____
_____

How Did I feel Before?

_____
_____
_____
_____

My Practice/Workout

_____
_____
_____

How Did I Feel After?

_____
_____

Daily Yoga

Date:

Intentions/My Mantra

_____
_____
_____
_____
_____

How Did I feel Before?

_____
_____
_____
_____

My Practice/Workout

_____
_____
_____
_____

How Did I Feel After?

_____
_____

Daily Yoga

Date:

Intentions/My Mantra

_____

_____

_____

_____

How Did I feel Before?

_____

_____

_____

_____

My Practice/Workout

_____

_____

_____

_____

How Did I Feel After?

_____

_____

Daily Yoga

Date:

Intentions/My Mantra

_____
_____
_____
_____

How Did I feel Before?

_____
_____
_____
_____

My Practice/Workout

_____
_____
_____

How Did I Feel After?

_____
_____
_____

Daily Yoga

Date:

Intentions/My Mantra

_____
_____
_____
_____

How Did I feel Before?

_____
_____
_____
_____

My Practice/Workout

_____
_____
_____
_____

How Did I Feel After?

_____
_____

Daily Yoga

Date:

Intentions/My Mantra

_____
_____
_____
_____

How Did I feel Before?

_____
_____
_____
_____

My Practice/Workout

_____
_____
_____
_____

How Did I Feel After?

_____
_____

Daily Yoga

Date:

Intentions/My Mantra

_____

_____

_____

_____

How Did I feel Before?

_____

_____

_____

_____

My Practice/Workout

_____

_____

_____

_____

How Did I Feel After?

_____

_____

Daily Yoga

Date:

Intentions/My Mantra

_____
_____
_____
_____

How Did I feel Before?

_____
_____
_____
_____

My Practice/Workout

_____
_____
_____
_____

How Did I Feel After?

_____
_____

Daily Yoga

Date:

Intentions/My Mantra

_____
_____
_____
_____

How Did I feel Before?

_____
_____
_____

My Practice/Workout

_____
_____
_____
_____

How Did I Feel After?

_____
_____

Daily Yoga

Date:

Intentions/My Mantra

_____

_____

_____

_____

How Did I feel Before?

_____

_____

_____

_____

My Practice/Workout

_____

_____

_____

_____

How Did I Feel After?

_____

_____

Daily Yoga

Date: _____

Intentions/My Mantra

_____
_____
_____
_____

How Did I feel Before?

_____
_____
_____
_____

My Practice/Workout

_____
_____
_____
_____

How Did I Feel After?

_____
_____

Daily Yoga

Date:

Intentions/My Mantra

_____
_____
_____
_____

How Did I feel Before?

_____
_____
_____
_____

My Practice/Workout

_____
_____
_____

How Did I Feel After?

_____
_____

Daily Yoga

Date:

Intentions/My Mantra

_____

_____

_____

How Did I feel Before?

_____

_____

_____

My Practice/Workout

_____

_____

_____

How Did I Feel After?

_____

_____

Daily Yoga

Date:

Intentions/My Mantra

_____

_____

_____

_____

How Did I feel Before?

_____

_____

_____

_____

My Practice/Workout

_____

_____

_____

_____

How Did I Feel After?

_____

_____

_____

Month:

My Yoga Goals This Month

_____

_____

_____

_____

What Can I Do To Reach my Goals?

_____

_____

_____

_____

My Progress

_____

_____

_____

_____

Feelings After Reaching my Goals

_____

_____

Daily Yoga

Date:

Intentions/My Mantra

_____
_____
_____
_____

How Did I feel Before?

_____
_____
_____
_____

My Practice/Workout

_____
_____
_____
_____

How Did I Feel After?

_____
_____

Daily Yoga

Date:

Intentions/My Mantra

_____
_____
_____
_____

How Did I feel Before?

_____
_____
_____

My Practice/Workout

_____
_____
_____

How Did I Feel After?

_____
_____

Daily Yoga

Date:

Intentions/My Mantra

_____

_____

_____

_____

How Did I feel Before?

_____

_____

_____

_____

My Practice/Workout

_____

_____

_____

_____

How Did I Feel After?

_____

_____

Daily Yoga

Date:

Intentions/My Mantra

_____
_____
_____
_____

How Did I feel Before?

_____
_____
_____
_____

My Practice/Workout

_____
_____
_____
_____

How Did I Feel After?

_____
_____

Daily Yoga

Date:

Intentions/My Mantra

_____

_____

_____

_____

How Did I feel Before?

_____

_____

_____

_____

My Practice/Workout

_____

_____

_____

How Did I Feel After?

_____

_____

Daily Yoga

Date:

Intentions/My Mantra

How Did I feel Before?

My Practice/Workout

How Did I Feel After?

Daily Yoga

Date:

Intentions/My Mantra

_____
_____

_____
_____

How Did I feel Before?

_____
_____
_____
_____

My Practice/Workout

_____
_____
_____

How Did I Feel After?

_____
_____

Daily Yoga

Date:

Intentions/My Mantra

_____
_____
_____
_____

How Did I feel Before?

_____
_____
_____

My Practice/Workout

_____
_____
_____

How Did I Feel After?

_____
_____

Daily Yoga

Date:

Intentions/My Mantra

_____
_____
_____
_____

How Did I feel Before?

_____
_____
_____
_____

My Practice/Workout

_____
_____
_____
_____

How Did I Feel After?

_____
_____
_____

Daily Yoga

Date:

Intentions/My Mantra

How Did I feel Before?

My Practice/Workout

How Did I Feel After?

Daily Yoga

Date:

Intentions/My Mantra

_____
_____
_____
_____

How Did I feel Before?

_____
_____
_____
_____

My Practice/Workout

_____
_____
_____
_____

How Did I Feel After?

_____
_____

Daily Yoga

Date:

Intentions/My Mantra

_____
_____
_____
_____
_____

How Did I feel Before?

_____
_____
_____
_____

My Practice/Workout

_____
_____
_____
_____

How Did I Feel After?

_____
_____

Daily Yoga

Date:

Intentions/My Mantra

How Did I feel Before?

My Practice/Workout

How Did I Feel After?

Daily Yoga

Date:

Intentions/My Mantra

_____

_____

_____

_____

How Did I feel Before?

_____

_____

_____

_____

My Practice/Workout

_____

_____

_____

_____

How Did I Feel After?

_____

_____

Daily Yoga

Date:

Intentions/My Mantra

_____
_____
_____
_____

How Did I feel Before?

_____
_____
_____
_____

My Practice/Workout

_____
_____
_____
_____

How Did I Feel After?

_____
_____

Daily Yoga

Date:

Intentions/My Mantra

_____

_____

_____

_____

_____

How Did I feel Before?

_____

_____

_____

_____

My Practice/Workout

_____

_____

_____

How Did I Feel After?

_____

_____

Daily Yoga

Date:

Intentions/My Mantra

_____
_____
_____
_____

How Did I feel Before?

_____
_____
_____
_____

My Practice/Workout

_____
_____
_____
_____

How Did I Feel After?

_____
_____

Daily Yoga

Date:

Intentions/My Mantra

_____
_____
_____
_____

How Did I feel Before?

_____
_____
_____

My Practice/Workout

_____
_____
_____
_____

How Did I Feel After?

_____
_____

Daily Yoga

Date:

Intentions/My Mantra

_____
_____
_____
_____

How Did I feel Before?

_____
_____
_____
_____

My Practice/Workout

_____
_____
_____

How Did I Feel After?

_____
_____

Daily Yoga

Date:

Intentions/My Mantra

_____
_____
_____
_____

How Did I feel Before?

_____
_____
_____

My Practice/Workout

_____
_____
_____

How Did I Feel After?

_____
_____

Daily Yoga

Date:

Intentions/My Mantra

_____

_____

_____

_____

How Did I feel Before?

_____

_____

_____

My Practice/Workout

_____

_____

_____

How Did I Feel After?

_____

_____

Daily Yoga

Date:

Intentions/My Mantra

_____
_____
_____
_____
_____

How Did I feel Before?

_____
_____
_____
_____

My Practice/Workout

_____
_____
_____
_____

How Did I Feel After?

_____
_____

Daily Yoga

Date:

Intentions/My Mantra

_____

_____

_____

_____

How Did I feel Before?

_____

_____

_____

_____

My Practice/Workout

_____

_____

_____

_____

How Did I Feel After?

_____

_____

Daily Yoga

Date:

Intentions/My Mantra

_____
_____
_____
_____

How Did I feel Before?

_____
_____
_____
_____

My Practice/Workout

_____
_____
_____
_____

How Did I Feel After?

_____
_____

Daily Yoga

Date:

Intentions/My Mantra

_____
_____
_____
_____

How Did I feel Before?

_____
_____
_____

My Practice/Workout

_____
_____
_____

How Did I Feel After?

_____
_____

Daily Yoga

Date:

Intentions/My Mantra

_____

_____

_____

_____

How Did I feel Before?

_____

_____

_____

_____

My Practice/Workout

_____

_____

_____

_____

How Did I Feel After?

_____

_____

_____

Daily Yoga

Date:

Intentions/My Mantra

_____
_____
_____
_____

How Did I feel Before?

_____
_____
_____
_____

My Practice/Workout

_____
_____
_____
_____

How Did I Feel After?

_____
_____

Daily Yoga

Date:

Intentions/My Mantra

_____
_____
_____
_____

How Did I feel Before?

_____
_____
_____
_____

My Practice/Workout

_____
_____
_____
_____

How Did I Feel After?

_____
_____

Daily Yoga

Date:

Intentions/My Mantra

_____
_____
_____
_____

How Did I feel Before?

_____
_____
_____
_____

My Practice/Workout

_____
_____
_____
_____

How Did I Feel After?

_____
_____

Daily Yoga

Date:

Intentions/My Mantra

_____

_____

_____

_____

How Did I feel Before?

_____

_____

_____

_____

My Practice/Workout

_____

_____

_____

_____

How Did I Feel After?

_____

_____

Daily Yoga

Date:

Intentions/My Mantra

_____
_____
_____
_____

How Did I feel Before?

_____
_____
_____
_____

My Practice/Workout

_____
_____
_____
_____

How Did I Feel After?

_____
_____

Month:

My Yoga Goals This Month

_____

_____

_____

_____

What Can I Do To Reach my Goals?

_____

_____

_____

_____

My Progress

_____

_____

_____

Feelings After Reaching my Goals

_____

_____

Daily Yoga

Date:

Intentions/My Mantra

_____
_____
_____
_____

How Did I feel Before?

_____
_____
_____

My Practice/Workout

_____
_____
_____
_____

How Did I Feel After?

_____
_____

Daily Yoga

Date:

Intentions/My Mantra

_____
_____
_____
_____

How Did I feel Before?

_____
_____
_____
_____

My Practice/Workout

_____
_____
_____
_____

How Did I Feel After?

_____
_____

Daily Yoga

Date:

Intentions/My Mantra

_____
_____

_____
_____

How Did I feel Before?

_____
_____

_____
_____

My Practice/Workout

_____
_____

_____

How Did I Feel After?

_____
_____

Daily Yoga

Date:

Intentions/My Mantra

_____
_____
_____
_____

How Did I feel Before?

_____
_____
_____
_____

My Practice/Workout

_____
_____
_____

How Did I Feel After?

_____
_____

Daily Yoga

Date:

Intentions/My Mantra

_____
_____
_____
_____

How Did I feel Before?

_____
_____
_____
_____

My Practice/Workout

_____
_____
_____
_____

How Did I Feel After?

_____
_____

Daily Yoga

Date:

Intentions/My Mantra

How Did I feel Before?

My Practice/Workout

How Did I Feel After?

Daily Yoga

Date:

Intentions/My Mantra

_____
_____
_____
_____

How Did I feel Before?

_____
_____
_____
_____

My Practice/Workout

_____
_____
_____
_____

How Did I Feel After?

_____
_____

Daily Yoga

Date:

Intentions/My Mantra

_____
_____
_____
_____
_____

How Did I feel Before?

_____
_____
_____
_____

My Practice/Workout

_____
_____
_____
_____

How Did I Feel After?

_____
_____

Daily Yoga

Date:

Intentions/My Mantra

_____

_____

_____

_____

How Did I feel Before?

_____

_____

_____

_____

My Practice/Workout

_____

_____

_____

_____

How Did I Feel After?

_____

_____

Daily Yoga

Date:

Intentions/My Mantra

_____
_____
_____
_____

How Did I feel Before?

_____
_____
_____
_____

My Practice/Workout

_____
_____
_____
_____

How Did I Feel After?

_____
_____

Daily Yoga

Date:

Intentions/My Mantra

_____
_____
_____
_____

How Did I feel Before?

_____
_____
_____
_____

My Practice/Workout

_____
_____
_____
_____

How Did I Feel After?

_____
_____

Daily Yoga

Date:

Intentions/My Mantra

_____

_____

_____

_____

How Did I feel Before?

_____

_____

_____

_____

My Practice/Workout

_____

_____

_____

_____

How Did I Feel After?

_____

_____

_____

Daily Yoga

Date:

Intentions/My Mantra

_____
_____
_____
_____

How Did I feel Before?

_____
_____
_____

My Practice/Workout

_____
_____
_____

How Did I Feel After?

_____
_____

Daily Yoga

Date:

Intentions/My Mantra

_____

_____

_____

_____

How Did I feel Before?

_____

_____

_____

_____

My Practice/Workout

_____

_____

_____

_____

How Did I Feel After?

_____

_____

_____

Daily Yoga

Date:

Intentions/My Mantra

_____

_____

_____

_____

How Did I feel Before?

_____

_____

_____

_____

My Practice/Workout

_____

_____

_____

_____

How Did I Feel After?

_____

_____

Daily Yoga

Date:

Intentions/My Mantra

How Did I feel Before?

My Practice/Workout

How Did I Feel After?

Daily Yoga

Date:

Intentions/My Mantra

_____
_____
_____
_____

How Did I feel Before?

_____
_____
_____

My Practice/Workout

_____
_____
_____
_____

How Did I Feel After?

_____
_____

Daily Yoga

Date:

Intentions/My Mantra

How Did I feel Before?

My Practice/Workout

How Did I Feel After?

Daily Yoga

Date:

Intentions/My Mantra

_____
_____
_____
_____

How Did I feel Before?

_____
_____
_____
_____

My Practice/Workout

_____
_____
_____
_____

How Did I Feel After?

_____
_____

Daily Yoga

Date:

Intentions/My Mantra

_____
_____
_____
_____
_____

How Did I feel Before?

_____
_____
_____
_____

My Practice/Workout

_____
_____
_____
_____

How Did I Feel After?

_____
_____

Daily Yoga

Date:

Intentions/My Mantra

_____
_____
_____
_____

How Did I feel Before?

_____
_____
_____
_____

My Practice/Workout

_____
_____
_____
_____

How Did I Feel After?

_____
_____

Daily Yoga

Date:

Intentions/My Mantra

_____

_____

_____

_____

How Did I feel Before?

_____

_____

_____

_____

My Practice/Workout

_____

_____

_____

_____

How Did I Feel After?

_____

_____

Daily Yoga

Date:

Intentions/My Mantra

_____
_____
_____
_____

How Did I feel Before?

_____
_____
_____
_____

My Practice/Workout

_____
_____
_____

How Did I Feel After?

_____
_____

Daily Yoga

Date:

Intentions/My Mantra

_____
_____
_____
_____

How Did I feel Before?

_____
_____
_____
_____

My Practice/Workout

_____
_____
_____
_____

How Did I Feel After?

_____
_____
_____

Daily Yoga

Date:

Intentions/My Mantra

_____
_____
_____
_____

How Did I feel Before?

_____
_____
_____
_____

My Practice/Workout

_____
_____
_____
_____

How Did I Feel After?

_____
_____

Daily Yoga

Date:

Intentions/My Mantra

How Did I feel Before?

My Practice/Workout

How Did I Feel After?

Daily Yoga

Date:

Intentions/My Mantra

_____
_____
_____
_____
_____

How Did I feel Before?

_____
_____
_____
_____

My Practice/Workout

_____
_____
_____

How Did I Feel After?

_____
_____

Daily Yoga

Date:

Intentions/My Mantra

_____

_____

_____

_____

How Did I feel Before?

_____

_____

_____

_____

My Practice/Workout

_____

_____

_____

_____

How Did I Feel After?

_____

_____

Daily Yoga

Date:

Intentions/My Mantra

_____
_____
_____
_____

How Did I feel Before?

_____
_____
_____
_____

My Practice/Workout

_____
_____
_____
_____

How Did I Feel After?

_____
_____

Daily Yoga

Date:

Intentions/My Mantra

_____
_____
_____
_____

How Did I feel Before?

_____
_____
_____
_____

My Practice/Workout

_____
_____
_____
_____

How Did I Feel After?

_____
_____

Daily Yoga

Date:

Intentions/My Mantra

_____

_____

_____

_____

How Did I feel Before?

_____

_____

_____

_____

My Practice/Workout

_____

_____

_____

_____

How Did I Feel After?

_____

_____

Daily Yoga

Date:

Intentions/My Mantra

_____

_____

_____

_____

How Did I feel Before?

_____

_____

_____

_____

My Practice/Workout

_____

_____

_____

_____

How Did I Feel After?

_____

_____

Daily Yoga

Date:

Intentions/My Mantra

_____
_____
_____
_____

How Did I feel Before?

_____
_____
_____
_____

My Practice/Workout

_____
_____
_____
_____

How Did I Feel After?

_____
_____

Daily Yoga

Date:

Intentions/My Mantra

_____
_____
_____
_____

How Did I feel Before?

_____
_____
_____
_____

My Practice/Workout

_____
_____
_____
_____

How Did I Feel After?

_____
_____

Daily Yoga

Date:

Intentions/My Mantra

_____

_____

_____

_____

How Did I feel Before?

_____

_____

_____

_____

My Practice/Workout

_____

_____

_____

_____

How Did I Feel After?

_____

_____

_____

Daily Yoga

Date:

Intentions/My Mantra

_____
_____
_____
_____

How Did I feel Before?

_____
_____
_____
_____

My Practice/Workout

_____
_____
_____
_____

How Did I Feel After?

_____
_____

Daily Yoga

Date:

Intentions/My Mantra

_____
_____
_____
_____

How Did I feel Before?

_____
_____
_____
_____

My Practice/Workout

_____
_____
_____

How Did I Feel After?

_____
_____

Daily Yoga

Date:

Intentions/My Mantra

_____
_____
_____
_____
_____

How Did I feel Before?

_____
_____
_____
_____

My Practice/Workout

_____
_____
_____
_____

How Did I Feel After?

_____
_____

Daily Yoga

Date:

Intentions/My Mantra

_____

_____

_____

_____

How Did I feel Before?

_____

_____

_____

_____

My Practice/Workout

_____

_____

_____

_____

How Did I Feel After?

_____

_____

Daily Yoga

Date:

Intentions/My Mantra

_____
_____
_____
_____

How Did I feel Before?

_____
_____
_____
_____

My Practice/Workout

_____
_____
_____
_____

How Did I Feel After?

_____
_____

Daily Yoga

Date:

Intentions/My Mantra

_____
_____
_____
_____

How Did I feel Before?

_____
_____
_____

My Practice/Workout

_____
_____
_____

How Did I Feel After?

_____
_____

Made in the USA
Las Vegas, NV
18 February 2022

44123989R00063